Gilligan

The Fat Boat Cat

Written by Alexa Shanafelt

Illustrations by Hailey Shanafelt

Meet Gilligan!

Gilligan is fat.

He lives on a boat.

He is a cat.

Gilligan is...

a fat boat cat.

Where has Gilligan cruised on his boat?

Gilligan's boat has cruised the West coast of the United States.

It has cruised the East coast of the United States.

It is cruising in Mexico now.

Gilligan's boat is a...

West-East-Mexico cruising boat.

What does Gilligan look like?

Gilligan has blue eyes.

He has lots of fluffy fur.

He has a long tail.

Gilligan is...

a blue-eyed,

fluffy-furred,

long-tailed

cat.

Does Gilligan have a best friend?

Gilligan's best friend is Doug.

His best friend is golden.

His best friend is a dog.

Gilligan's best
friend is...

Doug the golden dog.

Does Gilligan have a nickname?

Sometimes Gilligan is called Chonk.

Sometimes he is called Chub.

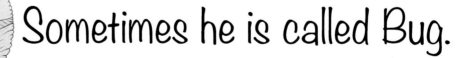

Sometimes he is called Bug.

Sometimes Gilligan is called...

Chonky, Chubby-Bug.

What does Gilligan do all day?

Most of the day Gilligan rests.

Then he naps.

Next, he sleeps.

Gilligan is...

a resting, napping, sleeping cat.

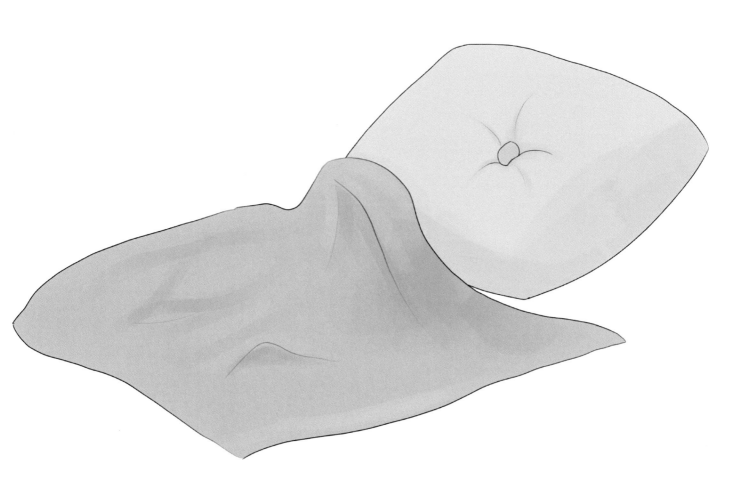

What else does Gilligan do?

Gilligan explores the docks.

He roams the beaches.

He wanders the marinas.

Gilligan is...

a dock-exploring, beach-roaming, marina-wandering cat.

What does Gilligan love?

Gilligan loves riding in the small boat.

He loves exploring in the small boat.

He loves sniff-sniffing in the small boat.

Gilligan loves...
riding, exploring and sniff-sniffing

in the small boat.

Where does Gilligan like to be?

Gilligan lounges in big boxes.

He squeezes into little boxes.

He finds all the boxes.

Gilligan is...

a lounging, squeezing,
box-finding cat.

Does Gilligan protect the boat?

Gilligan protects the boat from birds.

He protects it from fish.

He protects it from lizards.

Gilligan is...

a bird-fish-lizard boat protector.

What makes Gilligan cranky?

Once, Gilligan fell into the water.

He got wet.

He swam.

He was cranky when he got out.

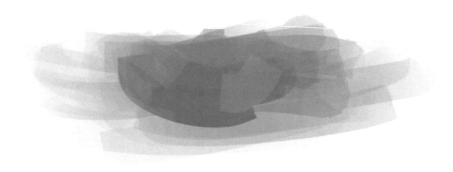

Gilligan was...
a wet,
swimming,
cranky cat.

Where does Gilligan hide?

Gilligan sneaks into the cupboard.

He hides in the engine room.

He crawls into hidey holes.

Gilligan is...

a cupboard-sneaking,

engine-room-hiding,

hidey-hole-crawling cat.

What does Gilligan do in big waves?

Gilligan sleeps in the sink when the boat cruises in big waves.

He meows when the boat cruises in big waves.

He pouts when the boat cruises in big waves.

Gilligan is...

a sink-sleeping, meowing, pouting cat when the boat cruises in big waves.

What does Gilligan eat?

Gilligan eats tuna.

He eats cheese.

He eats spaghetti.

Gilligan...

is a tuna, cheese, spaghetti eating cat.

Does Gilligan like his people?

Gilligan follows his people around.

He talks to his people.

He sometimes licks his people.

Gilligan is...

a following,

talking,

licking cat.

Is Gilligan happy on a boat?

Gilligan snuggles
with his people.

He purrs when he
is petted.

He loves

living on

a boat.

Gilligan is...

a snuggling, purring, loving cat.

Hi, I'm Gilligan! I have lived my whole life on Nordhavn boats in the United States and Mexico. I have two human sisters and one human brother. My human mom and dad cruise with me too.

I have met dolphins, iguanas, pelicans, manatee, and many other boat cats and dogs. My mom writes a blog about our boating adventures. You can follow us at www.mvnoeta.com. You can also see my videos on my YouTube channel 'Gilligan The Fat Boat Cat'.

Have a question? Just want to say 'hi'? E-mail me at Gilligan@mvnoeta.com.

**Follow
Gilligan the Fat Boat Cat
online!**

#gilliganthefatboatcat

Text Copyright © 2020 Alexa Shanafelt
Illustrations Copyright © 2020 Hailey Shanafelt
All rights reserved.
ISBN: 9781708738518

This book was written by Gilligan's mom.
The illustrations for this book were created digitally by Gilligan's sister Hailey, using Procreate

Made in the USA
Columbia, SC
08 May 2021